MATTER

kuhl house poets

edited by JORIE GRAHAM *and*

MARK LEVINE

MATTER

Poems by BIN RAMKE

University of Iowa Press, IOWA CITY

To Cynthia —
in anticipation of friendship
Bin
Spring 2006

University of Iowa Press, Iowa City 52242
Printed in the United States of America
Design by Richard Hendel
http://www.uiowa.edu/uiowapress

The University of Iowa Press is a member of Green Press Initiative
and is committed to preserving natural resources.

Printed on acid-free paper

Library of Congress Cataloging-in-Publication Data
Ramke, Bin, 1947–.
Matter: poems / by Bin Ramke.
p.   cm. — (Kuhl House poets)
ISBN 0-87745-900-2 (paper)
I. Title.   II. Series.
PS3568.A446M38 2004
811'.54—dc22   2004040742

04 05 06 07 08 P 5 4 3 2 1

for Nic *and* Linda

and

Lloyd B. Ramke

(1919–1984), chemist

I thought: You should not stop there.

That is not the place to come to the end.

PHILIP K. DICK,

The Transmigration of Timothy Archer

CONTENTS

ACKNOWLEDGMENTS

American Letters & Commentary: "Work in Silence"

Boston Review: "Thou Hast Blessed the Work of His Hands"

Bridge: "Reading a Line by Leyb Goldin"
"Thou Shalt Not Love by Ways So Dangerous"
"Variations on Lamentation"

Double Room: "Where the Famous Wish They Had Lived"

Electronic Poetry Review: "The Naming of Shadows and Colors"

Elixir: "Inarticulate"
"How Small a Virtue Was It?"
"A Hint of Mercy in the Weeds"

Fence: portions of "This World's Exuberant Surface"

Laurel Review: "The Tender Grasses of the Field"
"Song of the North American Martyrs"

Place as Poetry: Poetry from the Western States:
"Ariadne," "Rusalka," and "St. Alphais" from "All Saints"
"Narcissus Old, Anyone Young"
"The Greek for *Touch* Also Meant *Kindle*"
"Origami"

Ploughshares: "The Fall / The Unthinkable"

Smartish Pace: "49 Views of Childhood"

West Branch: "Versions of Errors" under the title "Versions of Error, Eros"
"Consolations of Comparison"
"After Virgil"

1

*The things of which there is seeing and hearing and perception,
these do I prefer.*

—Heraclitus of Ephesos, *Fragment 55*

THE TENDER GRASSES OF THE FIELD

When I was a saint I did not have visions but I could see and did note the color of the world—mainly gray, variations on dirt. It's ok, you can live here. The clean sky to attend the child whose hand is empty and mind is muddled.

Consider that earth is made of earth, a mineral and organic amalgam—beyond a tiny range, color is rare. Oh, they will tell you a particular plant, for instance, is red, that certain stars are red, but look for yourself. The color of fox, the color beneath the skin as platelets race, whirling alone in danger, for home.

What won't we do for the sake of the nerves, white threads of agony under the skin, on it, of it. . . . in the wake of remorse we need to pronounce bigger than names. Maybe a verb. Every saint knew how to keep custody of the lips.

The view is lovely, nice sun going, a mountain it goes behind, the mountain made of rock and all. Et in Arcadia Ego, you know. A sheep here or there. A cow. Water. The sound of water if not water. The sound of sheep if not the smell. You call it home.

THE QUESTION CONCERNING TECHNOLOGY

Proclaim thin anger through angelic flittering
among dials and diodes: we who witness
turn science sensible. The boy who was once
a boy takes his medicine, sleeps surreptitious

through the day, schools himself in stray
regulations, regularities. He schools himself
in light. In sweetness. Weathers serotonin,
luxuriates—from *luxuriare,* to be excessively fruitful.

From serum, from the Latin for whey, from
serom, fluid. To become the monster is to risk
revelation—silence suggests, if there were silence,

if the words would stop turning into words
in his silent in his spinning silence: from
the Lithuanian *spéndžiu,* to lay a snare.

CANONICALLY CONJUGATE VARIABLES

In a certain window as I passed a Shepherdess
watched from her painting, held her staff and stared
with a delicate stiffness out across the backs
of sheep—she was painted in Peru, and is of Peru
in many ways while here she hangs on a nail in a shop.
There is no Latin for "brown" or "gray."

And after the rain—and it is after, it does now seem
the rain is truly stopped, not like the teasing pause
that was a trap before—the glister of post-Carnival
beads in the bare late-winter limbs and strung across
wires and woven into the singular look of a wet city,
this is the moment after

        after that boy did casually
yet auspiciously touch the back of the girl
while walking home in this city in that rain
in a similar light to now which roared about
their innocent heads. . . . they were young, not
their fault. They will never do it again.

And then from my window at the hotel I watched
a taxicab catch fire, the astonished passenger
struggled with his bag and I could see from my privilege
a flame reflected in the gutter, the clean rain residue.

"For fools admire and love everything more
which they see hidden amid distorted words,
and set down as true whatever can prettily tickle
the ears and all that is varnished over
with fine sounding phrases." So Lucretius
attacking Heraclitus. "Dyed with an attractive sound."

The air made visible by rain,
the cars' wake crossed the sidewalk
to lap at the steps of my hotel.

ASTRONOMY FOR BEGINNERS

In such a sky a moon seems narrow but behind this sliver the full moon darkly
lingers—this light enlightens not, neither does it cheer: Dearer Reader, here it
says, this earth says, Choose your own Adventure—as if options were at hand:
when stars align we watch then wander luminous realms aghast and
anguished; or we might happily whistle, wistfully choosing choosing—there
was a clearing in the woods behind the house where he grew up, he would
walk prodigally there, a son with his dog where power lines hummed to
themselves and the sun and he would not hear nor heed but perhaps his dog
could hear the pitch of electrons tuned starlike unearthly and above, his small,
his bowed small head. He did hear other ecstasies, he did know dread, not of
the forest but of the coming home after. We remember the days, don't we,
when men walked on that moon, not the flimsy arc up tonight, but the full,
rich moon of the past, the moon strong nations raced to reach, the one the
Russians wanted, too: no one but that boy, perhaps his dog, remembers why.
Glitter of sun, the nearest star.

49 VIEWS Of CHILDHOOD

But he was a quiet child, I was, he was never
one, such a one as would wander

into wilderness alone—untrue, he was
one to play at death as boys will.

I was small when I was small and then
I was no longer. Dolls are delicate. Legs

and arms articulate to sit them
around you and tell them stories, to have them

tell you stories tell him stories make them
up. Dress them. If an end comes

it will come the sky will remain sky
and weather will be simple, simply

where we live during it. Another version
of this world engages these little ones

around us, about our feet, small humans
who have forgotten the future who

splash happily as if weather were a cure
for childhood. We didn't, he didn't, know

better than to sulk heavily as if
I did not watch secretly gathering

clouds, gathering under them
into likely groups—action figures. Us.

It was better when birds did not
gather so forcefully, mournfully back

before ravens and crows had moved
into cities following the pioneer

pigeons—boys walked under groups
would dismally look down, boys and blackbirds

crossing Sunday paths home
back before sparrows would

so cravenly eat from our hands;
children of today know only

small wishes and crooked feet,
articulated legs and artificial voices

to cry Mama or Papa at whim, at the least
tipping of self into horizontal. . . .

They do not see the green sky
we knew then, such empty grandeur:

in silence such insolence, solitude's
reward for being good, which is part

of every eros of childhood. In all parts
of this world there are children

except in the coldest southernmost,
Antarctica as imagined goal, to gather

there his dolls, my wish, his need
for clean weather and snow

articulated weather; is there no
child to sleep on that continent?

No child's dream floated ever above
the white horizon of an ice containment

bends the bodies to its will,
makes a wish. Like birds

the bodies fit in the fist. The still
children play those little games

the birds of the air the lilies
of the field, the insolence of the whole

agon; suicide as self expression
is paradox, as is sex as self. He made

little houses for his dolls to sit
through afternoons to peer

out narrow windows and be
invisible to have things to see.

I have, he has, things to say, he has
he had things. To say he was

a boy belonging to the end
of habitation, health, and happiness.

If this doll could sin she would sing
to him I would sing also, to her

is it like forsythia, logical because
the branch wavers and blossoms bloom

while wind does what wind will?
A dance is like this: to console

as to clasp these hands, touch there
in the air away from bodies

and then to angle the arms, turn
the hips and some part submerges

drowned as the doomed self would
like voodoo, dolled up and doomed—

dancing anyway ever. He could sing
and does deliberately, the child, it

follows that anguish is not me,
nor do we suffer who make those cries.

He would drown his dolls slowly
slide into agonized waters

which reflect the intricate lace
of the bridge which trembled above

them, a bridge which fell in the end
vortex shedding and resonant

oscillations, a dance the bridge did
with the air, not the words the wind

is the reason for suffering. A past
is anything's childhood is a reason

flares into mind like burning
burning which might have been

mind, a doll could have one
and could dance like anything.

VARIATIONS ON LAMENTATION

1

In those days in the capitol we who were interested
in such things would gather on stormy afternoons
to talk and watch the changing sky across the river.
It was a large river then, not so muddy as now,
with vast flocks of herons wading the far shore.
The green of cypress and palmetto some days
would glisten after a storm in such a way
that argument would cease, and we would drink
silent toasts to the light. Nevertheless, we hated
each other with such intensity no one
would shed a tear at the funerals, until finally
I alone am left to mourn, or not, the last
of my old companions.

2

Her company was, you know, delightful
except for those moments when
her eyes would fill and the room would empty.
Later, when we heard the silence return,
we would, too, and she never
mentioned a word about it but would take up
conversation like you would
knitting, except of course for the fact
there was one more on the growing list
of subjects to avoid.

3

There are three distinct layers of tears
when the eye is in good order: a layer as wetting agent
on the cornea itself; the middle layer, the familiar
salt-water solution; and a third, oily layer to retard
evaporation. The balance among the three is delicate
and essential, and astonishing.

4

Make dust our paper and with rainy eyes
write sorrow on the bosom of the earth
                      Richard II

5

No one denies the erotic potential
of her silent weeping, how desire
grows unbounded with each
heave of her shoulders,
how the slippery glistening
tracks down her cheeks
must be traced, tracked
by an erasing finger.

6

We have all heard the expression "the weight
of years," yet years have faint substance,
cannot be accurately measured

except in the trivial sense. Weight
would be a comfort, a relief, a positive
joy when compared to the anguishing
nothing which squeezes out our tears
during the night, which causes us to wake
on wet pillows even though we thought
we were dreaming happy as children.

7

It is a curious thing, a child is born
able to do some few things: suck,
breathe, piss and shit and weep
with such intensity he cannot
be ignored. Really there ought to be
a special word for this crying
of the newborn, more anger
than lamentation, filling
the house with anguish. The only adults
with such intimidating tears
are the divas—remember Rusalka.

8

I was never a surrealist. My work
has no glass tears glued
to a stylish face. I want the dust
to gather over time, the face streaked
from real sins, not clever pain.

9

A small broken heart is the cliché
by which we live with the weight
of our years. Even as small boys
we had a sense of what was in store,
inevitable if unbelievable.
The corner of the handkerchief
with which we wiped away the tears
(which were nothing but the effect of wind
from standing too long on the porch looking
for something on some horizon)
had some girl's initials embroidered.
Satin-stitch, so called. Cotton floss.

WHERE THE FAMOUS WISH THEY HAD LIVED

parmenides of elea

Where his influence could accumulate, where the horizon might retreat, where the basilisk smiles and the necessary arrogance of desire lingers into evening while yet hiding among the hieroglyphs. But I like it this way, he said to himself. Here shall I close my trustworthy speech and thought about the truth. Henceforward learn the beliefs of mortals, giving ear to the deceptive ordering of my words, he said. He watched stars move a certain way, the small sprinkling of the past he walked beneath when he was out late and lingering.

In a land of ha-has and paths of desire. Where Nothing hovers invitingly above the closest horizon. Between the angles of incidence and of reflection. Among the agonies in the garden. Elsewhere.

sigmund freud

"If his lips are silent, he chatters at his fingertips; betrayal oozes out of him at every pore." And yet looking into the mirror otherwise known as morning otherwise known as night was not a revelation to him. He had a path, strewn with candy wrappers, or flowers, and lined with stones, which was a comfort to him when his throat ached and his head betrayed him. Still wouldn't it have been good to stop in at some familiar coffee shop, to order in a childhood language a childhood treat, something with chocolate and a little something to soothe the guilt which follows from having hoped too fervently and made all those promises. A place where the libraries do not contain your own books and the children are not afraid. Memory, remember, is a dynamic process like the eloquence of birds and the kinds of cancer which affect the jaw. The cave of the mouth from which words emanate, and breath. "I am still out of work and cannot swallow," he wrote after the first of his thirty-three surgeries.

Emil Kraepelin

"In dream I was a child—*childhood* is our myth of psychiatry, but children continue to live in dream—being chased across a landscape. I was not afraid—there is no fear in such landscape—but I did hurry. I would live there where there are no shadowy mountains, where rivers are slender gleams and cold, where the grasses vastly sound through the evening, sounding of air known as wind, felt—but there was a barrier, a glass wall under which a child's body might fit, but not his head. There is no child in this world but in the world of dream I want to live there, there on the other side. I want to live in someone else's dream, any healthy child's. I will live in any body."

ALL SAINTS

Ariadne

If the stained things of the earth lie, as in
lie, and a thread on the floor is remarked,
there's a story to tell but not the one
that leads out, only, for instance, beginning,
or to begin again leads in, torn from
elsewhere, now here, nowhere you know
but still the face rises as in dream and speaks
as in dream but that's a real child in the corner
small and weak and beginning
its own sort of threaded passage.

Now it makes you want to touch only
surface, a blind tongueless traveler
when the word alone is witness to all,
the word which comes out of lung from
an act of breath and constriction of
the various parts of the throat—the breath

a thread dissolving on its way out—
a child out of the warmth into the world
ready to be fed, ready to listen: Listen,

Rusalka

Dvorak told this story: another creature of water
wants to be mortal (to have sex with a human), needs
permission from her father to die; there she sits

beneath the inconstant moon she sings
an aria for him which asks the moon to say
Mine are the arms that shall hold him, That between
waking and sleeping he may Think of the love that enfolds him.

This mortality allows us to touch one another and thread our way out into
bluish air and tinted anemones persistent in our paths, temptation and a kind
of hunger

saint Alphais

which only some can resist—hunger's catastrophe of touch—remember
Alphais' inedia, her gift of subsistence on only the host, the wafer of bread
received daily. To waste to essentials is one form of grace. Having lost her arms
and legs, living in a lean-to next to the church—these legends grow beautiful
in their cruelty, a thread thrown to the drowning, a sound which enlightens,
even hunger quivers bird-like within the mouth

> *imitating with the mouth the birds'*
> *liquid sounds came before men could delight*
> *their own ears by singing sweet songs (De Rerum Natura)*

sacrificial sanctity

The habit of hope saints evade, and the pettiness of life viewed from a certain
angle. Avoid the certain angle. If the air were flavored with lemon, say, or any
accidental floral that lines the walk, the habitual path from home
compounding the inarticulate with despair, the last remaining virtue one

learns with age to trust, to greet with a nod in the morning, ever waiting in the bathroom mirror, ready to carry on, to care. Among the things a long life teaches, none matter beyond a mirrored silvery way among the plants thick with insects eating each other into other forms, larva to pupa to the serial splendor of wings and delicate dining on nectar; such liquefaction of appetite can be learned in such a world can be learned by the singularly attentive, that the best birds are pigeons, next are sparrows; the full avian hierarchy founded on commonness—crows, boat-tailed grackles, etc. Nothing rare counts to the saint who has seen all things familiar and contained, who has seen and is content to see, and sigh. *I can do all that angels can*

Wallace Stevens

SONG OF THE NORTH AMERICAN MARTYRS

The child with too many mothers lived among
his many selves like a fox among chickens,
sleeping through all those little lives, waking only
to pain or passion that made a noise. A music.

Anaximines is said to have said, all things are air—
rarest it is fire, thicker it is wind, more thick, cloud;
further condensed, air is water, falling from cloud,
falling into fire then windily rising as steam—
but in its most arduous state of intensity, air is earth,
air is stone, and who could deny such a solid-state
physics. And yet the soul, he said, is air, and soul
holds us, frail humans, together—the persistent breath
is me, in and out is self, on cold days visible, on hot,
I feel my touch. But rarest of all airs is music. A
voice a victory

        and voice mumbles into the microphone
every chance it gets—it lies, will defraud incessantly
given half a chance. Elements of uttering include
false making, material alteration, legal efficacy
and intent, passing or making use; all this lying
caresses the lips and tongue, muttering tenderness.
Consider, for instance, the word *suture*. Utter it.
The wind cannot be repaired, it can be torn, it can tear.

*

These are several sounds at the serenade.

Cough, a mortal engagement, sympathetic vibration
around the deathbed: relatives gather solemn
as Bach on the organ, as the Art of the Fugue,
as a sigh, echo, a consolation to the living:

perjury is a pleasure; listen, word against word,
given, taken back. The echoing silence is not silent
there tearing itself against the self the wick the flame
furious with itself the heated particles pulling against
the charring wick. Perjury is false swearing, it is
the voice vacillating, it is the necessary music of
despair and reconciliation. Call and response.
Take my word for it.

                                        Uttering
a forged instrument is the passing or making use of a
forged writing or document with knowledge of its forged
nature.

        A name is a prediction. See the expectant
parent consulting the lists, studying meanings
to declare to a world, to give up her child as. . . .
I predict a you, o my child. A childlike spectacle
announced to being then utters itself as if
as if as if . . . I predict "you" will still be "you" next time
I say this name. I pronounce you into being, or out.

Speak softly, say little. Here are some names: Albert
DeSalvo, David Berkowitz, John Wayne Gacy, Jeffrey
Dahmer, Wayne Williams, Richard Ramirez.

Failing which, simply
failing, a small man such as Any would tender
a bounded ambition (to breathe, cough, sneeze, speak,
declaim, defame, denounce, announce, call, respond,
reply or merely in a small space out of the wind to
blow breath warmly into my own wintry hand) and
hand it over reservedly, to consume a self enraged,
in rags, or emptied, like pity.

Ite, missa est, the priest muttered,
and out we went with an organ intoning around us,
we were called a congregation who listened to
some hand at the keyboard, the machine a lung
wheezing—a building as if burning, embers floating—
and hope continued that we would be delivered
from the hand that hates us.

ACTION FIGURE

Every chemistry has a history—methylene blue,
we watched it change—aniline purple became
a pretty name and a color. A name is about

the sound it makes. A life, too. Here is a theory:
". . . severe arterial inflammation made
Dr. Thom's last years an agony for his family.

With his circulation impaired, he underwent
the amputation of a foot and lost memory
of all but the earliest years of his life. . . ."—

"Rene Thom, 79, Inventor of Catastrophe Theory,
Dies," (George Johnson, the *Times*). Any
body can have ideas, there are plenty. And

there are many ways to suffer, not all
of which are art. Lightly he thought the story
of wreckage as the clean ring of pages, pages

unaccounted—reading a book is like a thought
and a poem if it is warm and the light persists
into evening when sounds fly

where music and pictures fly through air flying
through our bones where the mind is breakable—
thus his theory of hope unaccountable.

HOW ONE PICTURES THE ANGEL OF HISTORY

Walter Benjamin

The visual is vibrant—molecules thin
like wheat bend, succumb to, like the,
the breath, breathing of the, the very air . . .

all that can be seen can be touched. No one
knows except through skin. A man lives
through the wish to be other than himself,

a woman lives equal to these, her limits . . .
should there be a window where she works
children of her neighborhood might

be heard through the glass glimmer: voices
vibrate; photons at a different speed spend
their lives circular and a shade of blue

virtuous as all get out, getting out a world
while some lingerer watches. Is it an art,
what we do when she's not watching?

She paints. She will sleep and we like
to think she dreams of light which heats
the beaches of southern France, some place

we've not seen, have not been to see.
She knows the light like the back of
her hand which moves (the light) (her

hand moves) before her (it holds the brush)
it moves before her but she does not
see, it is a kind of wing, her hand, flight

is a way to watch, angles, angels an idea
of wings, giant (*insect* from *secare*, to cut)
like newly hatched and ravenous.

She paints the wings red, cadmium red wings
flowerish, petals open from the back
of the boy who loves her, he of paint and she

of need created; there is a past to the painter,
not to the paint. Or, there is a past to mere paint
but a simple one, flat, not to the painter

who makes through the night makes
it up (her past) from books and borrows
wings from Fra Angelico; paints through

the night and makes it up from her life-
so-far worn bride–like a veil (her life so far)
before her, behind her in the mirror

(in front reflecting a narrowly focused
past) passing through the present as if
through the eye of a needle. *Cadmium*

red is basically cadmium yellow (cadmium
sulfide) with some selenium added in place
of sulfur. The element selenium, delightfully

named for the moon, was discovered in 1817—
the same year as cadmium—by the Swedish
chemist Jöns Jacob Berzelius—(Philip

Ball, *Bright Earth*). Another name
for color is time. There is an ink—drawing
is more intimate than paint, painting—

iron-gall ink produced by crushing and soaking
gall nuts of various trees in water to extract
the acids . . . ferrous sulfate and gum Arabic

added . . . commonly used from fifteenth
through eighteenth centuries . . . such ink
changed over time under pressure of light

from black to brown, the same brown as
bistre . . . the natural acidity—tannic and
gallic acids—eat the paper, ultimately

destroy themselves. Bistre came from trees,
too—the soot of various firings soaked
in water, filtered, yields a lovely ink—

burning chestnut gives a golden brown,
birch, a brownish yellow. *Bistre*, from
the Old Norse for angry, fierce, like the angel

of history, grim; from *biester*, having lost
one's way in a dark and dismal wood
at the mid-point of one's life, when an angel

as from the pen of Tiepolo, whose Doubting
Thomas too was drawn in bistre, an angel—"ink"
from Greek for *burn*—in brown descends to save you.

THE GREEK FOR *TOUCH* ALSO MEANT *KINDLE*

You must have noticed that curve, that jointure of neck
to shoulder, less gaudy than some angles and bends of the
body, a subtlety verging on arrogance especially when
a gleam, light—sun or candle—touched just as she turned
her head to catch you looking, to catch, like an angler
who misses the fish's mouth and instead, catches your eye.
Epicurus said there is matter and there is void: matter
we know by senses, void by conjecture. Sensation tells us
the world moves, and pleasure is possible. It is good
to know. It is a hand, mine, which wishes to touch her cheek.

I live now in a city of morning glories
(called bindweed where I used to live)
but here they caress the chain-links of fences
which are mainly void, and the solid of brick
which are the faces of buildings turned to us
who wander these streets. On days without sun
these flowers persist until afternoon, their color
deepening, purpling like bruises, a flesh
offered to any passerby, a kind of slow blaze,
a blue incineration of self like breath held.

THIS WORLD'S EXUBERANT SURFACE

1

Gracian: "we cannot see clearly
the things of this world, save by
considering them conversely
to what they are." This world being
the only one, one lonely consequence
resolves and solves for itself: embodied
drama of the word: what they are
things are is all we can safely say—
no, no safety there: are things?
And the lyric shape of the flock flying
flings itself into another appearance:
then a lyre, now a fan opening.
Graceful flirtation in the sky—what
color is this air? Just because invisible
does it follow it does not have color?
Oh green today, tonight the stars
spell some things ancient, Aristotelian
and delirious. This world is good
enough for some, better
there is never enough, never
a nextness sufficient to tell
"what happened?"

    Well, for instance, the birds
continued metamorphosing. They resembled,
reassembled into shapes and would shunt
desire into oblivion. Observation:
they crossed a sky and descended
onto a common horizon.

Next came
a color of the air, next the rain
and the day moved on—day
being a convention of design,
day being the accident of sunlight
grinding against a turning world.
This one.

2

Did you wonder that *miracle* and *smile*
emerged from the Latin *mirus*? A mirror
is a monument. "While Yet a boy
I sought for ghosts," said Shelley, but
my sly glance at every shiny surface
looks for evidence of me—distant, younger
than the current self, more admirable.
The modern city as ghost-trap
with glass angles and ever recurring
images floats a flicker at the edges
of vision: glass houses hover.

Note to himself: "Read up
on the manufacture of mirrors"   Walter Benjamin

3

The Chief Carpenter made three screens for Morita Shiryu to paint—
large screens entitled "Dragon," "Tiger," and "Emptiness," words
conveying similarly weighted perceptions of danger and promise.

*As the hierarchy of prime causes declines toward Nature, Soul comes
between intelligence and Nature. . . . The highest Position in Nature
goes to Heavenly Bodies and Time, and the lowest to sensible matter.*
    Dennis Brand, *Liber de Causis*

     *

Architecture as toy as fatal presence. To experience architecture is,
full size, too fragmentary. From a distance—
see, the people like ants, like figures of the modeler's
model village—reduced to table-top dimensions,
something we can see we must
see whole. Otherwise at street level we merely walk though doors
and look through windows.

A room on the twenty-fourth floor induces a feral sense
of watchfulness: the city sparkles to itself oblivious
of inhabitants (fleas on the elephant); here and there
a watcher blinks to see the pouring lines of headlights
as pattern moving, beads strung on wires of intention
and distance—and the windows illuminate themselves,
bright arrogance.

Above even this is the airplane, a modern form of delay
and isolation, a kind of induced error made of metal
and burning oil, as is everything in the city, of it.

Anything will ring if struck with the proper hammer.

4

From I Ching: *six at the top means*
the prince shoots at a hawk on a high wall.
He kills it. Everything serves to further.
A man always carries a magnet because he needs to know
what is the world made of even as it moves:
carries also a compass which must be shielded from the magnet;
carries a tape measure which shows automatically diameters
of pipes, or any rounded thing, like stems or limbs;
Above, fire;
below, the lake.
And the image haunted the day
and that night as he tried to sleep the fire
still twisted above and below mirrored
and he did not know whether he slept or kept
awake watching burning like the fire the fire
burning as if burning the lake. The very water
which is also what makes the world. What is not
magnetic is often alive, not always. Tricky.
Like sex which is made of signs and signals
and is rarely what it began to be.

Not every burning is a lake, but below the burning
is vision, often, if reversed. A man is a map. No.
Here it is burning flowers, they rise writhing,
rather pretty. They are of many kinds, few attract
metals—a man and a woman might be a kind of fire
and lake, hard to know the difference.

       *

The true miracle was walking on mirrors.

       *

The flimsy flowers rise and writhe, righting themselves
above the dirt no matter what the seed's position—
anabasis, a facing of the light. The scent
of flowers flung into an airy fascination. He would hold
his magnet to the stem to check, just to be sure.

It is burning flowers. It is raining metallic
compounds, the ore of metals rise along veins
of molten world. This world I mean, the one
you're standing on.

5

The earth's condition is receptive devotion.
Thus the superior man who has breadth of character
Carries the outer world.
Which is the sun's, the outer, the world.

*

And in the modern mode she suffered—
How amazing that she could be killed
by her own skin, her own skin and the sun.
I cannot commend this Bible to believers,
but we wicked find solace here.
In the dark the terror and angels come
so let's have something to tell them, words

*

to the ghastly messengers, *a bird
of the air shall carry the voice and that
which hath wings shall tell the matter.*
If another name for "past" is "future"
then all converges toward random
allegories: this is what pain means
to teach time and time again flares

*

across the marshes of a past
burning, they could have been,
they might have meant something. What filled
her nights was night, not the chemistry
of petroleum, the wounded, wounding
earth itself bleeding. She loved like land,
yes, and longed to be a mother of nations.

Likewise also these filthy dreamers defile
the flesh, despise dominion, and speak
evil of dignities—Jude 1:8. Tremendously

saddened, burdened by a self in the world
she sliced an escape, a space in her own body.
If tears work, do work, if it helps to cry, or
whether or not she noticed, she left, leapt into

the saturated future called The Fullness
(sliced, as in the body opening or the squeezing shut
of eyes—the body thus broken, healed open)
of Time

       "What does the body mean by
trembling or crying?" asked M. Derrida.

6

To ward off, something like danger
(let's give it a name) or reward
anger, or rename the words we make
when crying, trembling, shivering, all the little
dances the skin will do, (and the inner parts).
Left too long in the refining sun, the flesh
has its own devices—darkening across the
face, the little map changing, islands of melanin
and the lingering lives below the surface
of mind and matter, hastening to renew—I was
one of those children, too—we watched the flares
across the marshes, the anonymous hydrocarbons burning,
methane, history, little dots of light distant;
while the family car pursued home we whispered

stories about the light, making them up, our selves.
Nothing is true but the stories. What more. What
more is there to die of? The light of the eyes
but you must open your eyes someday,
no one's allowed to live darkly today.
We thought we brought it all along,
eyebeams, back in one of the pasts, now
we know better than the light that the light
the light of the eyes rejoiceth. But buildings
are best for prayer that have the least light—
To see God only, I goe out of sight:
And to scape stormy dayes, I chuse
An everlasting night   John Donne

7

There are curious desperations in this world:
hours and years later I remember kissing a certain
one and does she remember? She said:
There is no word more beautiful
than, oh, say, *parfait*. Maybe *algebra*.

Some truth is true up to four times ten to the fourteenth power:
Euler's reply to Goldbach:
That every even number is a sum of two primes,
I consider an entirely certain theorem
in spite of that I am not able to demonstrate it.

The lucky get a good view through leaves
of a tree out there beside the window and maybe
in fall the leaves turn tender colors and maybe
there is distance made visible.

A curious desperation in the world
is distance made a material manifestation
of what looks awfully like a future,
something to link the long afternoons into years
which pile up like disks on spindles, a thing mathematical

on spindles a thing mathematical out of a parable
the one about the end of the world arriving
as the last gold disk settles onto the last of three
diamond needles all according to an elaborated
(*Es Scheinet wenigstens, dass eine jede Zahl, die grosser ist*
als 2, ein aggregatum trium numerorum primorum sey.
        Christian Goldbach)
all according to an elaborated set of rules;
the lucky learn the rules—another version of luck
is to know other stories while through your window
you watch whatever falls fall like rain like snow
(A mirror is a monument)
like rain like snow at different speeds meaning
rises from the mud beneath the feet of boys
and girls walking past if you lean you can see
them down there *thinking* is the word the usual
(*Meanwhile the whole history of probabilities is coming to life, starting*
in the upper left-hand corner, like a sail   John Ashbery)
word *reflecting* is the word passed into what

they think of as the future which from
this perspective might be. It is good
to aspire to the life of the lucky
(A mirror reverses momentum)
it is good to be ready to pretend
you've been there before; luck as a symmetry —
as anyone in a mirror knows not to shatter
the illusion the crazed surface
(*There is no place that does not see you*   Rilke)
the crazed illusion of surface serves
when the little spaces collide and
the contrary computations
get you nowhere. A mathematics
will serve, and any mirage (there are truths true
up to four times ten to the fourteenth power)
will serve and a mirror will lead them like
a little child. Out the window a face peers back
wondering where it came from, the word *miracle*,
which is how to stand on the world.

NARCISSUS OLD, ANYONE YOUNG

We were subtle dancers, this world and I,
when we were in love forever, ever
moving across the surface of
the other's eyes
                  resist this mirror's
glitter which keeps us intricate
and a little cruel but ready to gather
into arms an infinite remorse,
a sad seduction reduced into one last
smile a life spent waiting. With the slender tip
of her tongue in your ear, how can you listen?
. . . *and though beguiled be not betrayed*   Lucretius

          There was a time we listened
like Echo, tried to be each the other,
learned to build cities and cemeteries, architecture
and architects, tried for order; in our intrigue never
guessed we could ever be other than lovers.

If only I could speak, what words I would say!
The surface of the pool wavers in wind, weaves
confluence into vision, into such humor
as the face which must be seen—
beguiling shiny hooks the fish seek out
hidden in shoals of littler fish hiding.

THOU HAST BLESSED THE WORK OF HIS HANDS

He was the one who would not use his face —
would keep it in reserve, would use his hands,
one at a time, alternately. Would use feet.

Would be happy when it suited, would
mourn when required. Such a poem as was
needed, he would make. Would want,

when those he loves are in pain,
to be. There. To bleed for all equally.
And here was a thing to believe: "to live whole

lives with littleness, how tired it makes us,
a sharp fear, this point to which the eye was
drawn — defames then defeats the hand — an agony

it is to follow self into its shameful needs" and
so forth. "Wherever you can: count" said
Francis Galton. We do not know most things.

I might know a few things. I can
rarely tell the difference. Where there are flocks
of Monk Parakeets, Green Neighbors, they rouse

us to collect feathers under streetlights
on nightly walks where are builded unsightly nests.
A dozen wild parakeets in furious formation fly

across the park swerve to streak past, accidental, me.
Pyromancy, a method of augury by reading
weblike patterns which appear on bone surface

following the application of heat, especially
favored in China—but what did it sound like
when the bone cracked, its surface crazed?

The sound of the word "sound," as in "the sound
of young girls." Or "the voices in my head."
Complex looking, calligraphically.

Among things to love in this world are eyelet fabrics,
suggestive nests of absence promising
a glimpse of flesh and remembrance of touch,

of the feel of the young world.
The skin beneath the fabric shines—
Wann was a word for it, for gloss or sheen; *Fealo*

meant glint, the sparkle of sun, say, on waves;
while *lux* meant the source of light, *color*
the effect of that light on a surface, as of

the moistening skin beneath the eyelets.
Lumen, the ray of light traveling between
the surface and the eye, the source and

the surface; *splendor* was the word for
that final reflected, lustrous quality,
that which draws the hand inexorable.

"The winds sweeping the surface
of the waters diminish them, as does
the ethereal sun unraveling them

by his rays." *De Rerum Natura* 5, 390
When an electron "moves" to a higher orbit
it does not move but merely is now elsewhere—

once it was here, now it is there. This is not
possible in the old world where I used to live
by manufacture. The new world is one of

probabilities, where numbers add up
and the glint of sun on flesh is ephemeral.
All is diminished in his world, yet all the more

unaccountably glorious. We love it all,
and each the other, or so it seems. His hands
cracked a sound a second face fallen.

2

For nothing is harder than to distinguish the real things of sense
From those doubtful versions the mind readily provides.

—Lucretius, *De Rerum Natura*, 4:467–68

INARTICULATE

When the winsome inducements of *res*
derilecteur deflected his adult assuredness
he played with the doll left in the cab, he on his way
somewhere, the doll out of nowhere and never
returned to its child. How ordinary. Things
without masters might save us:

the metaphor of the poem as doll, as an imitation child
to be played with and learned from—
of the poem as Pinocchio,
as homunculus, as little mind-machine
which takes after Daddy and Mommy
but behaves according to its own,
to its inner necessity, is a convenience.
A way of articulating. And the arms and legs do move.

The man in the taxicab holding each hand
as surreptitious dance staring into the face
the doll's face a kind of anonymity. Unkind.
To play is to turn self into a place
of playfulness, to be open to the needs
of a kind of delirium. Like a stage.
Like chemistry. Unlike any child's ownership.
To become a form of absence which whistles
windlike and forlorn after the trudging
of grotesque articulations, mimetic movements.

He put it in his briefcase and changed his life.
He lived happily ever after. I made him up.

HOW SMALL A VIRTUE WAS IT?

We did love: our parents, our pets,
and all the lesser creatures of the night.
We might fear our own dreams.

Here are the games we would play: Blind,
to be led unharmed but frightened
by companions; Lost, to go alone

and friendless in the world; Statues, to be flung
into awkwardness, hardened there;
Hide and Seek, to hunt or be hunted,

to be found, therefore to lose.
For never is there a least of what is small,
but there is always a less . . .

There is always a greater than what is great
equal to the small in number, but with regard   Anaxagoras,
to itself, anything is both small and great.   frag. 15

Every child plays Orphan, some out of envy,
some out of fear, and every child knows how
who has awakened in the dark, who has slept.

But this is a better future, warm, and the light
continues long into the evening, the sounds
of neighbors give comfort and there are tiny

pieces of music and data and pictures
flying through the air flying through your
very bones the machine.

WORK IN SILENCE

How does one determine
which is his right hand and
which his left hand?
How do I know my judgment
will agree with another's?
—Wittgenstein

My right handed mother cuts
paper patterns
paper my mother in the night cutting
patterns my sister wearing paper
in the night the needles glitter

the pins hold the paper on my sister
her body
she wears
herself in the night holding
in the night a writing
a darkening delivers us
a darkness then a dawn

they work through the night there is urgency
they are clothed in urgency it is their work in the night
they speak rarely the rustling of the paper could be the sound
of the words printed thereon words on my sister
on the paper she wears and dotted lines and arrows

a thin figure I
read long into the night I cut
paper strips of paper I read

someone puts paper into the tree onto the trees
in the night the trees bloom paper long
strips white nothing more beautiful streams
like tears in the night like light

we should make sounds we should use air
to make sounds you hold the mouth this way
you breathe out through it it usually works
there is a name for it

see here her
hand like light descends
below it a shadow ascends
see they touch

not a shadow it is
her other hand sinister
the needle pierces

the other hand receives
no word my mother speaks
nothing to the other hand to come
receive

my sister's dress the fabric
like air moves with air
the air breathes this dress
it is light

and two blades converge
the sound they make is a hiss
a small shrillness the scissors
a mirroring against the paper first
like Narcissus the blade touching itself

—a mirror the window has become
it shows the boy himself
me my face breathing there are no
words coming out of it—

desperate to reach its other self
then the cloth to cut the tiny cry

some old air still
caught in her wings she
balances awkward looking but
balanced
it is a morality a way to let live

how the word "believe" works is
you accept the unstated penumbra
of impossibility and then con
struct there a camp of consolation
in other words
in the house
angelic as if the hierarchy held
as in held water
something between Man and God, Mom
as if any word were
tenderly merciful—man—god—mom

what woman could live there her winged
wisdom bearing her onward
her uses of air : to breathe :
to swim in, as if : to shape glittery :
to hold in trust a shape until it returns

in the night their four hands wing shaped
I see them reflected in the window
against the dark air waiting

or here is the other mode to appraise and approach:
the house as a kind of box and form of failed weather
it is warm for instance or cold it contains us all boy
girl mother at some time or other we live there it is
home and some are away from home and some have
never been home and some move forever as if the
fullness of time were our roof the fall our foundation

A HINT Of MERCY IN THE WEEDS

Ann Lauterbach

As if there were options we do complain
heavily about the weather, the first of the ways we
intrigue each other. Another is the fabulous despair
neurosis brings, the cavalier approach to encroachments
tellingly arranged: if some are happy around us,
others are not, but the differences are demurely subtle.
Fabulous is an interesting notion, and the child at
my feet twirls—it is a dance, yes—at the saying of it,
eager little thing she is, full of dance, full of
regal splendor, if you look for evidence, for the light.
Can this continue, this biology which makes a child
your little duplicate, which makes children make
incremental progress until they grow, as we say, up,
never then or again to be happy, flinging themselves
toward the unknown, the intensest of futures,
happy only in retrospect? The weather is theirs, too—
every child knows not to complain. Oh
woe, you might say, for all the good. Oh woe is
everyone, more or less. Yet still she elaborates there still
engaged with herself, her blood her bones her little
delirious body parts, each full of its own weather, all
splendid in gorgeous subordination, in delight.

CONSOLATIONS OF COMPARISON

On the shape and scale of cloud: the airplane enters the cloud
like sex—how so? Tenor and vehicle, the man said. The shape
of the airplane (the cloud has no shape like the good man.) The
cloud does not enter the airplane, we seal the windows who look
from leisure into the color of water, dust, and distance. The light
is still faster than we are we think hard the soft cloud is sliding
past like sex.

Vehicle. Plato would speak of lover and beloved, no mutual balance
but all desire on the one side all desired on the other—what a clear
world it seems before entrance, after exit.

The allegory of the man in the marketplace who spoke and turned to
hear his echo, the molecules bounded off the surrounding structures—
temples, bathhouses, banks—and returned formulaic to his spiraling
ear. Real spires of sound cling to the moist grass out there where there
are fields and smallish creatures, a rumbling.

His mother prayed he would forget.

From the radio escaped the story of an inventor of the world's most powerful
microscope under which the lonely Man of Science placed a drop of water
and in that drop a world—temples, fields, and a young woman, dark hair
curling like desire in the eye of the watcher who follows her little life falls in
love with her there she writhes in agony his love his only love dries under the
microscope vapor rising unseen it was science fiction a kind catastrophe of
language which echoed in the boy's dark room his radio clinging to air sealed
against.

THE FALL /

Was wir nicht denken können,
das können wir nicht denken;
wir können also auch nicht s a g e n
was wir nicht denken können
                    —Wittgenstein

A bewilderment,
his wilting sense of betrayal, a wilderness—

he composed the history of his own privacy.

If you can't imagine it you can't think about it;
you can't talk about what you can't think about.

He is a small man and maybe a child.

What I miss most about horses is the entangled sound and smell—
how they exhale into the feed trough explosively searching out
the last of the grain, winnowing;

Why could I not remember the word "hackamore"?

This horse could crack the head of the boy rider;

The child was frightened of animals;

among the animals which frightened him: horses, cows, chickens,
squirrels, pet rabbits, a calf we kept for fattening. I was not afraid
of birds or snakes.

"You can't say it that way anymore."

There are ways to whistle for it,
the thing: the word calls the concept to heel.
But the word has a mind of its own.
Go whistle, it says.

"A man named Flitcraft had left his real-estate office, in Tacoma, to go to
luncheon one day and never returned."

I wish I could write a story. Can stories be written? Is it
that Echo and Narcissus (an instance) just *is* —
that all telling and all writing is pointing? Can you
think up a new one? Another instance

the story about the child who went injured to the hospital and
when he awoke after anesthetic one eye was gone.

Is it a story "about" or a story "of" — or can you only say "story"

as in "Story: a child goes to the hospital led to believe he is to have
(just like his classmates have had) his broken leg repaired who awakens
to find one eye was removed under the bandages
is a hole where once was wholeness." Tell that one.

All lost things have the same voice.

The Leo House a place I would stay in New York when I was young
and poor and could sleep under a Jesus nailed there was a man
next door in 4-J "My name is Forget — for jay — a room for a tryst.
What's my name? Don't forget."

It is undeniably beautiful that mirror, miracle, and smile are derived from the same word—anyone can see that. There was no mirror in that room, few smiles.

"5.621   The world and life are one.
5.63   I am my world. (The microcosm.)
5.631   The thinking, presenting subject; there is no
           such thing."

But there was a boy riding a horse by a bluff, the day, and the danger invisible—what were they thinking? His thoughts had minds of their own. His thoughts strayed the horse had a body and mind. Don't forget he was thinking and who trusts the words anyway? They have minds of their own?

"   If I wrote a book, 'The world as I found it',
             I should also have therein to report on my body
             and say which members obey my will and which
             do not, etc."

The member which obeys—or what is philosophy for? For boys and obedience, forbearance—the member which will not obey, has a mind of its own.

Imagine a son named "whistler."

(What is the German for "whistle"? What is the English? We could look it up. How often brilliance and blindness collaborate. [Consider the Hebrew for "stream."] (blind, *bhlendh*-to glimmer indistinctly, *brillare*, sparkle) whisper whine whistle, all the same *preifen, die pfeife, der pfiff, das* . . . . *männliche Glied.* The obedient little mind at ~~word~~ work.)

He wrote the word in German, the German for "member" is not the same word. There are words for words.

"   This then would be a method of
        isolating the subject or rather of showing that in
        an important sense there is no subject: that is to
        say, of it alone in this book mention could *not* be
        made."

The boy could ride along the bluff overlooking the coulee, the horse between his legs obedient and skillful, hoofs picking a way like wisdom itself inches from falling. The water was slow and brown the day too.

"5.632   The subject does not belong to the world but
        it is a limit of the world.

5.633   *Where in* the world is a metaphysical subject to
        be noted?"

When it was titled by later scholars, the Metaphysics was noticed to be next to the Physics, hence its name as sign of its simple place, what could be neater? Obedient in time, the place kept, a book, so to speak. Its own story. A book like a painter has a name, a person.

"   You say that this case is altogether like that of
        the eye and the field of sight. But you do *not*
        really see the eye.
              And from nothing *in the field of sight* can it be
        concluded that it is seen from an eye.

5.6331　For the field of sight has not a form like this:

Eye —  ”

"Echo:　Entire memory / hangs tree / in mind to see / a bird be"
　　　　　　　　　Robert Creeley

Imagine as someone's son a painter named "singer."

And again Creeley:
"Echo:　　. . . gone couldn't come
　　　　　　back what was with
　　　　　　it wouldn't come looking"

"5.634　This is connected with the fact that no part of
　　　our experience is also a priori.
　　　　　　Everything we see could also be otherwise.
　　　　　　Everything we can describe at all could also be
　　　otherwise.
　　　　　　There is no order of things a priori."

Even in his part of the world riding was a luxury
by this time, no longer part of making
a living, part of, an echo of, a kind of living looked at askance:
it was where he lived, not why. It was not necessary
and was a kind of story telling, an enactment like saying . . .

No one said ever anything first. It's a puzzle.

The boy would live and would return
the river would too

return. The river was twice and infinitely itself:
or is a river that which it contains, which is never the same
like, you know, fluxions.

To leave home, the injured boy left
whistling in the dark
with the eyes closed a way of being with the eyes
if you have eyes, still

whistling past graveyards it happens that change occurs
like wilderness won, won over, overcome.

/ THE UNTHINKABLE

Leaves, as of books, or that which is left
(the leave is worth half the fit, the tilers would say,
a kind of geometry the story of measured earth)
or the green turned to gold of the autumn.

All is a kind of coming. The boy behaved
himself and being good, was allowed to ride.
The fall was never his fault, nor the horse's.
Every story says the gods could have done other,
Es könnte auch anders sein, he said.

It could have been otherwise. He was a boy falling.

In the right light anything will shine, anything is
the measure of anything else. Beautiful is another word

for light. The waves and particles break upon the shore.
Imagine such a world.

He made a book of glass, blown
glass complete to read it was
to focus the pages would ring

if turned it was not necessary
to turn such pages the book
need never be opened it could be

read closed it need never change
anyone can read such a book
open or closed it recounts all

stories all events none it is
like a mirror when viewed against
a dark ground when held at

an angle it resists light is silent
reading of the book is like the clean
ring of the page

on the pages of the book
the words rested rode like
jetsam on the waves

wetted by the water but
free & forming patterns
various and changing

to turn a page was like
pouring the words mixing
words any story can be

told the stories continue
and who can see through
how many pages un-

every where
Echo or mirror seeking of itself
And makes a toy of thought
Coleridge

counted hundreds the
story of shipwreck and horses
and horror clouded water

along the river bank
the crumbling bluff the world
a small transparent terror.

VERSIONS Of ERRORS

They return from the movie to find themselves still clothed but in love. Suddenly she remembers that in 1956 her mother left the iron on when the family left for the movies one night. They had returned to a house which might have been a smoldering ash, a reduced mass of matter—the sadness of possibility is infinite and yet the swallows' paths in flight at sunset spiral ever more tightly.

I believe in the past the Japanese divided the day into twelve parts which they named for animals. And if the hour of the dog was the time to write letters, I would think it would be late, say ten o'clock modern time, dark in all zones, and the letter would fill with coy questionings, like the inconsequent warblings of birds disturbed by the dark. I should like a day like that.

She loved something so intensely she never failed to include it in anything she wrote. Whatever the ostensible subject, Stein wrote only about her love, her intensity of commitment turning language itself ecstatic under her tongue. Her tongue became a little bed, a pillowed redness upon which she would invite day and night the body of her love to lie. Lie to love, her body night and day.

Matter, from the Latin for material, stuff, wood, derived from *mater*, mother, orig. the growing trunk of a tree—the bark of a tree, too, is alive, especially the smooth such as aspen into which lovers like to carve by hand their initials, sometimes with entwined heart-shapes, and sometimes the tree is thus infected and if aspen the entire grove will die since they are all one tree manifested.

ORIGAMI

Consider how little a thing
it is, her hand.
How nothing is sufficient
but everything is necessary.
Wings, for instance.
Handkerchiefs. Umbrellas.
Folded things. Her hand
an enclosure. A secret space
enacted in the flesh, a false
interior. A touch.
And yet it is anguish to know
something about anyone, to feel
with one's own hand the hollow
bones so near flight. No one
can close his eyes on this:
a wonder, willfully offered
as if nothing, a mere mereness,
a trifle like a fan unfolding
of paper oiled to translucency.
Her skin was not transparent
only his breath upon it.

ON THE ORIGIN Of LANGUAGE

People longed to "understand"—come to terms with, we might now say—their unhappiness, which made them different from the not-unhappy animals around them. These not-unhappy creatures seemed to mock the struggling humans who, once they came into language, invented happiness and with it, a kind of childhood.

Another theory is that language invented the human by a mechanism not yet well understood. "Happiness" seems in this theory to play a catalytic role, not as fact but as conceptual possibility.

Finally there is the suggestion that the pressure of consciousness began to be too painful to remain merely interiorized, hence the process of exhaling was over time modified into a release not only of carbon dioxide and the fetid gaseous products of the decaying internal organs, but a release also of the parasitic entity best understood as "thought," or "arrogance," or "interior necessity."

PAIN IS THE HISTORY OF CONSCIOUSNESS

We are at war we are told. There is a god of it.
Is there a god of pain? We are in pain. You are
welcome to your own. You may
protest. A small bird —*passer*—

passes my window and its shadow
across the drawn shade is like a drawing
I once in better times displayed.

The light is a kind of passing like pain.
At war, and in light, and the bird flies
specter-like past my window which is luxurious
and full of future. Like an omen
a body is a poor excuse. Impoverished.

You know, pain. A war
rewards all small affairs. Air
and apples abound in this district,
happily for our comfort. We miss most
the small warmth of afternoons.
Recall a tidy elegance, specter of
when one was happier reading hints of what
to expect when the body bent unwilling —bends
unwilling to its task. Pain is
arrogant, dismissive, debonair.

AFTER VIRGIL

All through the precise butchery lungs
retained much of the last breath of the bull
like light waiting in candle wax—even when
tossed onto the altar there was the chance
to return to sound, song, lament,
a bellow of desire a residue of despair.

THE NAMING OF SHADOWS AND COLORS

I. Things That Cast Shadows

Dear, the world in its gentleness, in that
whatever can be taken must be shared,
such as umbrage; and the light
can be in your eyes or the shadow
on the page in such a way as obscures
the shape—casts shadows, detaches surface,
the varieties of shade seduce:
afraid of the shadows of doubt, of
my own dreams, yet I know dreams too
have names yet I cannot recall: Do
I dream in color? The color of the world
is the skin, isn't it—bound and bounded
trying always to escape itself, that was
the dream the world had, I had dreamed
it had a shape, a shade and semblance
. . . *semblances and thin shapes of things*   *De Rerum Natura,*
are thrown off from this outer surface   Lucretius
the sincerity of surface suffices as
if dream is a shadow cast by Mind
shading into itself, the little mind
making itself seem large in hope of frightening
itself into resolution; then dream is a kind
of color that light distorts, dissolves, discards.
But color is light, is the behavior of light
in the world. What is there to love
but the world, its things and shades and
matter. Let us love the names: what
is the name of this world? Space.

What is the name of the other world?
Time. What is the name of the light?
Color. What is the name of color? Change.
Image, as Lucretius contended,
is continuous, a crumbling into infinity
of everything, wave upon wave
of everything, gentle because too thinned
to threaten, attenuated everything . . .

The story used to be told, Pliny told
the story, lovely, of Dibutade   *Naturalis Historiae,*
outlining her lover's shadow on the wall   XXXV, 151–2
the night before he went to war. No one
tells stories anymore. No one casts shadows.
What did Pliny love? A good story. A story
is shadow cast by event, or by doubt,
or a story is the color of the absence
of the heroine, she who tacked the shadow
onto the wall, for instance.

My older brother, who became an engineer and helped men walk on the moon
took photography classes as a child I watched and listened his teacher made my
brother make a pinhole camera (I made one secretly myself, the salt-box and
tinfoil taped slyly into technology, a kind of making like love) and by the time
they got to enlarging I saw the darkroom duties as an identical process
backwards—these men organized light to send along a lensed new path to
collide with silver halides all light informed. . . . Although the structure of the
$AgBr$ and $AgCl$ lattice is face-centered cubic, an enormous variety of crystal
shapes can be obtained, depending on the number and orientation of twin
planes and the conditions during growth . . . the crystals in commercial

emulsions usually contain mixed halide phases. Films suitable for a hand-held camera generally contain silver bromoiodide, in which iodide ions are incorporated into the AgBr lattice during crystal growth.

www.kodak.com/US/en/corp/researchDevelopment/

And here is a story told of things:
that the thing names itself like for instance
when that other dream comes into your room
and pesters you for your things, all things,
as if things were lesser entities, smaller
than their colors, thicker than their shadows.
So I talked with her, my friend, who knows
Japanese, and asked her how to say things
what it might be like to say things as if
the shadow of my thoughts were cast across
half a world, the source of shining,
the orient, the language of the rising
sun (but see
how the word refers to resemblance,
"oriental topaz"—look it up)

. . . *so many words, too, are pronounced alike.*
"Kinkai" means "a gold bar," "the coastal waters,"   Malinda Markham
and "it gives me great pleasure (to do that for you)."

"Suited to simple races, peasants, and savages"
Le Corbusier—not his real name—said of color
which he found on his journey to the east.
Me, I like them all, all colors, shading

into each other, you know, the spectrum,
a spectacle of itself, oh like a ghost. Specter,
inspector Ball provides the names:

verditers: artificial copper blues
Mars colors: artificial iron oxides   Philip Ball,
lake pigments: from fabric dyes   *Bright Earth*
white—titanium dioxide
cinnabar—mercury sulfide (red)
cinnabar—blood of dragons and elephants—*According to*
Avicenna the dragon wraps his tail around the legs of the
elephant, and the elephant lets himself sink   Bartholomew
upon the dragon, and the blood of the dragon   Anglicus,
turns the ground red; and all the ground that   *De proprie-*
the blood touches becomes cinnabar . . .   *tatibus rerum*

Let's have it so. A good story

(*tolle lege, tolle lege* spoken in a sing-song voice by
an unseen child from behind a wall, according to Augustine)

whose riper abundance deserves the world's
gaudy spring, whose tender Pity might never
die, a famine of the grave, fairest bright memories,
from light's waste to sweet bright eyes
increase desire, self-substantial fuel—
gaudy the world, or else glutton: too cruel:
here are other names and things:
yellow ochre, ferric hydroxide
red ochre, Fe_2O_3, ferric oxide

heat yellow ochre and get red ochre
hydrate red ochre and get yellow
from the madder, a flower,
$C_{14}H_6O_2(OH)_2$, alizarin
$C_{14}H_5O_2(OH)_3$, purpurin.
They named the rainbow Iris.

A shadow of some former self,
down Ursulines Street thirty years later I
glimpse again—like a dream of stone—
the garden through the gate (if a hand
goes through, a gate, if not, a door)
as if in pity. As if pitied? Piety.
Pity the world, or else this glutton be,
To eat the world's due, by the grave and thee . . .
a vision of cloistral shade and floral
lined walks, a place forbidden but there,
in sight, temptation to our better nature:
From fairest creatures we desire increase.

2. Things That Have Color

THING [[ME < OE, council, court, controversy,
akin to GER *ding*, ON *thing* (orig. sense, "public
assembly," hence, "subject of discussion, matter,   *OED*
(how odd these ways of making words
have surface, to cast a form of selves upon

the page like the pen eroding into ink,
like shadows of the thinking that survives)
thing") < UE *tenk-, to stretch, period of time <
base *ten-, to stretch > THIN]]

If we scrutinize closely what is done in counting an
aggregate or number of things, we are led to consi-   Richard
der the ability of the mind to relate things to things,   Dedekind,
to let a thing correspond to a thing, or to represent a   *Meaning*
thing by a thing, an ability without which no think-   *of Number*
ing is possible.

Fast Color. Fast, as in the desert for forty days
and nights. How speedy the fast are, the girls
we admired in high school. Fastened to no one,
they were themselves and loved. Feast.

In a certain drawing by Tibaldi there is no wound
no place for the hand to insert itself. Hand made
belief, manufactured faith. Anyway, belief being
handy enough, a ready relief from the stress
of waiting for the tomb to open. After all it is
Easter today, is it not—the day I write.
This tree here, see outside my window, this
tree is full to bursting of its own efflorescence,
I see the embarrassed little knobs and
buds so full of their own sexuality oh
don't look, give it a little privacy.

What color will it be, this bloom when
the skin cracks and the petal emerges,
and what emergencies we have known
in their shadow necessities, there.

So this apostle wanted a place
to put his hand, to touch to taste to see
the wound. Wounds R Us this season,
this is spring, it says here. You
can hear the breaking bark
see the little cracks forming hear
the invisible screams as the flesh parts,
tears, molecular disintegration. It bleeds
itself into season. Who doesn't.
Touch the torn places.

"Mummy hand with amulets (human hand and
blue-glazed pottery, Late Period"—   The Field
—says something in sign,   Museum
the hand, I believe, the fingers. But in Egyptian.
Elsewhere another boy disregards the Saint—
a book in his sinister hand his severed tongue
in his right, severe witness to his own faith   "St. Romanus of
his own wound—below the boy's throat cut   Antioch," Art
in paint, Zurburan, a kind of storytelling.   Institute of
Everyone talks too much given half a chance.   Chicago
Dumfounding, such stillness observed, a moment—
let us observe a moment of silence. What color is it?

3. words neither cast shadows nor have color

Easter Monday, 2002:
All that was hidden is revealed,
and sometimes the thing was chocolate,
yet mostly you see the shattered shells
discarded, peeled off but reconstructable
of the boiled egg, the colors dizzying,
the sad detritus of the body of the res.

Shadow, shame and hand-tinting all have their
effects on how we say it: once the poets were first
and the painters to follow, to make only
what had been named: "Line drawing   Pliny
was invented by the Egyptian Philocles or by the   XXXV, 16
Corinthian Cleanthes, but it was first practiced by
the Corinthian Aridices and the Sicyonian Telephanes—
these were at that stage not using any color, yet already
adding lines here and there to the interior of the
outlines; hence it became their custom to write
on the pictures the names of the persons represented."

"Maple leaves are often used to convey the idea that you have been
jilted. The Japanese word for Maple leaves and love being iro—a
subtle reference to changing colour."
        C.G. Holme, *Glimpses of Old Japan*
        from Japanese Colour Prints: Birds
        and Flowers (London, 1936)

"Iro" does mean color, though: "Kami" is "paper," and
"irogami" is "colored paper." "Cha" is "tea," and "chairo"
is "brown" (tea-color). "-ppoi" is kind of like our "ish,"
and "iro" with "ppoi" attached (iroppoi) means "sexy,"
especially for women. "Colorish," in a way, but only non-
Japanese would hear it like that. If you put the same
"iro" with the character for "woman" or "man," it
means a lover. But "maple leaves" is just "momiji."

"Since the beauty of a Japanese print is mainly that of lines, straight or curving,
broad or slender, I do not see why a carver's knife is not at its best in nude
studies. The reason why, unlike the Greeks, we did not venture to find the
highest symbol of art in the human form, should be discovered in social ethics,
more than anything else, which taught us how to transform life's falsehood into
a hyperbole of superficial arabesque beauty."

The Ukiyoye Primitives, Yone Nocuchi (Privately Printed, Nakano,
Tokyo, 1933) p. 107

What have you named yourself?
Is it a secret? Is it dangerous?
Who is allowed to choose her own name?
What would your mother think?

The name of the species is a place
to start. Not a place. The birds he named
were sometimes wrong, the names, but
his pictures were of something—of the young
of the Whooping Crane, he named
Sand Hill Crane. I traveled there once,

Nebraska, the Sand Hills. I was late and the birds
would speak in the twilight, a kind of murmuring
loud and it had to do with sleep.
I would sleep, too, after the drive
from Chicago. There is a city in Colorado
not my destination, named Ovid.

Is there a place you practice
pronouncing this name, secretly? Is it
safe? Is it the same name in the dark
as in the light? Does it fade during the day?
Can you pronounce it backward?
Can you say it in your mind so loudly
it hurts? Can you live without it?

Audubon's Feliciana Sketchbook, 1821 to 23,
contains flying things mostly, not birds,
Praying Mantis, Spider, Fly, for instance,
this mantis was circus pink, the fly as if
dressed in blue-checked abdomen. The spavined
spider, full of venomous threat, gray and
yellow, enlarges on the page—I do not believe
he knew its name. I think he lied,
made it up with his eyes closed. Spider.
We must love such a world.
Among us still, they are elegant all,
pink and gray and blue. Ovidian charm—
those he named, like Arachne, like Picus.
Every name is holy. Hollyhock
whose lower leaves waver lacy with rot or

chewed into delicacy. It takes a little time for
the charm of the hollyhock as an adolescent scatter
of self into the willing world, tipping over
still standing florally abundant,
thickly raucous and weedish.

Or can it ever matter again who
tends the garden now that longing has deflected
itself into itself, selfish, now that the little ones
bask in the light, the litter of insect bodies
gathers nightly underfoot, under purple waves?
I prefer the moth, the bulge
of body awkward against the grace of wing;

who flies under moonlight and gathers
grace into himself, eats the flowers, or perhaps
(the gray insignificant) eats the clothes
off our backs, under our feet the wool
of our carpets. The good moths eat anything,
in one of their forms. Fancy. We have a world
we love one another. We can fly
in the dark, enough dark, desiring.
I am thinking of History, which is a way
to name time. The name of this year,
for instance. To be allowed, from *laudere*,
to praise. To name is to praise is
a trick of words, all words are tricks.
A picture is worth thousands. *Pingere*,
ut pictura poesis. Time absolves
everyone everything. Give it

time. Solves all problems. Loses,
sits it out. He made other sketchbooks
of flowered weeds and wilderness,
of every horned and horrific creature
he might see. Beast. That is a name.
Yours? Truly.

READING A LINE BY LEYB GOLDIN

The day comes to the door like a beggar

He was hungry and threatened and dying in 1941.
I know a boy who reads and no longer feels
hunger, lives in the shadow of the beggarly
day at the door. And his mother cannot cry
but has never had better cause—
the thinning shadow of day at the door.
He wrote: It is a hard thing to grow old
when you are still young. Like a day at the door
like a beggar. She cannot cry because
she cannot. The eyes are not our own
are poor creatures of the light
and so full of fluids as to be barely
above drowning in themselves—
the substance of vision is the tri-
partite tear, but when Percival Lowell stared
into his severe machine
he would see as the works of men
of Mars canals and streams mapped
before him, he would see, was seeing
his own delicate vessels of the retina
of his own eye, perhaps—profoundest
insight, a kind of joke the body plays—
imposed on the constant world
the inconstant self, its sight.

To see is to agonize
astronomy is to architecture as
poetry is to pyrotechnica
a long way home is a short way
everything is implicated
in everything else, or
nothing is nothing
self is discontinuous
there is no hunger
that does not haunt
remaining life
even if that life never
was as on Mars
even if no Martian
or his mother saw the shadow
growing old at the door like a day waning.

Vascular endothelial growth factors
which normally maintain healthy
blood vessels can lead to overgrowth
of vessels that obstruct vision. Further,
amaurosis fugax, fleeting blindness,
may occur from excessive clotting
of platelets. A man's own eyes
may defeat his vision, a woman's.
If the day is at the door can the night
be much delayed?

$C_{42}H_{50}N_6O_4S_2 \cdot C_4H_4O_4$
is the visible name of a drug
like any food compounded of carbon,
hydrogen, nitrogen, oxygen, a bit of
sulfur—can be a cure for consciousness
gone wrong. Not a cure but a respite.
Not forever but for now, which is like
forever except like the day
at the door, the beggar. Pain is the site
of the self—ah—now mind is under-
standable. It is the persistence of pain—

"the arrangement of the Psalms, which seems
to contain the secret of a mighty mystery,
hath not yet been revealed unto me"
wrote Augustine, known as Saint—
the vision of saints is famous sanity,
regards not the damage it does—
let us pluck out that which offends.
Yet still the day will stand by the door—
feel the warming the sun warming
the thin skin of the eyelids,
feel the warm tear on the cheek
the assurance that the kind world
is hungry only for itself
devours only itself
we are along for the ride, though.

THOU SHALT NOT LOVE BY WAYS SO DANGEROUS

John Donne

Disturbance in the Night

When we wake to it it
is as if we never were asleep
when we wake to it it cannot
happen that we shall ever sleep
again as the parent in the night
listens for the sound of a child
returning through the early watches,
the sound of a door opening and
relief floods it fails or falls
with clemency the passing passion
of relief it is so to know a body
which is bound to you in sleep
in dream then drear awakening.
It is so similar it is not always but was.

Lakeshore

The kinds of laughter available seen
hovering above his life, his little
Ovidian life, full of change and
under only simple spells and happy,
seemed would be available always, or
however many were plucked and plundered
a surfeit would remain, a certain
lifetime full, at least, as needed
to complete the promises made all
nodded complicit to and through which

only anguish would be believed
too limited in quantity to concern,
long nights and short days numerous
on the cumulous ledger, so unamusing.

Variously engaging the self the slow
engagement with the world again: a crisis
becomes a way things are—no more, just
yet another place from which to watch
waves wear themselves and shore into time—
any place along this lake to sit today—
yesterday was pleasure, today is habit;
standing its ground a gull calls
searingly—it could be anger
or maybe a courtly beckoning to some
dear appearing potential, a call to wake
as gulls wheel above me, a mass of them
not neatly but like insects whirring
going nowhere being alive menacingly
except of course it is the way it is, this
recourse to the world as menace, threat
of the world as world it surrounds us
ultimately drowning us in water, air,
some fluid like time itself threat
threatening full of nothing but
here is no wind, but there is air
overcoming its own indifference to enter
under the body's nearest need, lungs as
something like a duty, a dare, a divisive

habit to keep the self alive threatened
any excuse to keep a song-like self
like the skin of lake which moves by force of
the air which is only gray, and wet to touch.

bounded but infinite

What of it, what long agonies of it
we shared, we should have shared, would have
had we lived enough longer there among
small creatures and long nights and
darker intrusions into the child. I never
knew better than to keep moving
along, like the nice policeman said:
Nothing to see here. Pliny said
the power and majesty of the universe
at every turn lacks credence
if one's mind embraces parts of it only.
But even Pliny's mind could not hold it,
none can, we know. All minds minimal
reservoirs of the known, limitless only
in what is waiting, warning, soon to devour.

There are those who fear certain colors,
a particular, and who fear sharp
sounds more than knives. He removed
from his bed the quilt we gave him—
too green maybe, or too acute those angles
where the fabrics met unwholesomely.

A wish remains a book full
of further worlds being made
even as you stand there reading
or lie languid on your couch, turning
pages indifferently, back to front,
front to back like the tender grass.

CHEMICAL VIRTUE

Swiss violet, Methylene blue—names limit the languor of this world, its agony called appetite. You eat it, it changes color. You breathe it, it warms, returns to its turbulence more human, more anxious to please. Or so we, heroic and altering, wish. I like knowing something, but much is too much. When I learned that the shape of a protein was how other proteins knew to attach, I recognized the romance. She, walking toward me accidental on the sidewalk, has a shape. *Pluck from the memory a rooted sorrow* the man said—it was a question, can't you, or why can't you. ... . Erasure is the great desire, chemical and candid. Take and eat, this is my body. I noticed how neatly the clouds fit into those holes in the air, then I thought how the air is part of the cloud so there is no hole, just more of the same. And the sun breaks itself into little pieces which hurtle my way, enter my face through the lens, a little piece of me like water. It all becomes the Egyptian art decreed evil by Diocletian, chemistry, the old writings treating of silver, gold, and transformation; the darkness of the earth which is fruitful, even to excess, contrasts with the light color of desert sand, barren and beautiful. The name of a thing is the history of the thing—or the name and the history is the thing. Or, what does a boy want with history, such a toy, a chemistry set in his basement, a little Bunsen burner of his own alight, flickering, a golden hue against the wall, holy the vision.

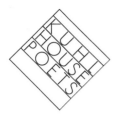